TREE

designed and written by Althea
illustrated by Barbara McGirr

Longman Group USA Inc.

Published in the United States of America by Longman Group USA Inc.
© 1982, 1988 Althea Braithwaite

Originally published in Great Britain in a slightly altered form by Longman Group UK Limited

ISBN: 0-88462-196-0 (library bound)
ISBN: 0-88462-197-9 (paperback)

Printed in the United States of America

88 89 90 10 9 8 7 6 5 4 3 2 1

Library of Congress Cataloging-in-Publication Data

Althea.
  Tree.

  (Life-cycle books / Althea)
  Summary: Illustrates how an acorn grows into an oak tree.
  1. Trees--Juvenile literature. 2. Trees--Life cycle--Juvenile literature. 3. Oak--Life cycle--Juvenile literature. [1. Oak. 2. Trees] I. McGirr, Barbara, ill. II. Title. III. Series: Althea. Life-cycle books.
QK475.8.A47   1988   582.16   88-13852
ISBN 0-88462-196-0
ISBN 0-88462-197-0 (pbk.)

Notes for parents and teachers
Life-Cycle Books have been specially written and designed as a simple, yet informative, series of factual nature books for young children.

The illustrations are bright and clear, and children can "read" the pictures while the story is read to them.

The text has been specially set in large type to make it easy for children to follow along or even to read for themselves.

This oak tree is
already hundreds
of years old.

It gives food and shelter
to many small animals.
It is their home.

4

Green acorns are hidden
among the oak leaves.
They are nuts,
the oak tree's seeds.
When they are ripe
the acorns will fall
from the tree.

Thousands of acorns
fall each autumn.
Many are eaten by birds,
squirrels and other animals.

Animals carry off acorns
to eat when food is hard to get.
They hide them in the earth,
but some are forgotten.

Winter is over and
spring comes.

A forgotten acorn splits.
Its root grows down
into the damp earth.

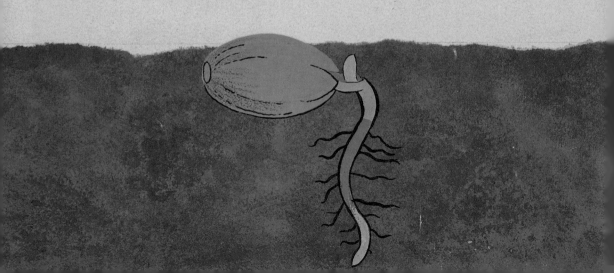

A shoot, or stem, grows up.
The first pair of leaves
opens in the spring sunshine.

In its first year, the seedling
grows about twelve leaves.

When winter comes,
the plant takes back
food made by the green leaves.
The food, stored in the tree's roots,
will help it grow next year.

Now the leaves are dead,
but they stay on the tree.
They protect the tiny buds
getting ready for spring.

It is spring again.
The last dead leaves fall.
Tree buds burst open
as the new leaves unfold.

Each year the young oak grows
and is taller and stronger.
Now it has branches.

Slowly, slowly, the tree grows.
Its trunk is strong and straight.
Its branches spread out.

Under the ground the roots
spread out too.
They keep the tree from falling.
They collect water from the soil
to send up to the leaves.

The leaves use air and sunshine
and water to make the food
the tree needs to live and grow.

After many years of growing,
the oak will start
to make its own acorns.
The male flowers hang in clusters.
Their pollen is carried by the wind
from tree to tree.
It falls on the small female flowers
growing among the new leaves.

18

The female flower grows
in a little cup.
It is a flower with no petals.

After a flower is pollinated
an acorn starts to grow.
It is protected by the cup
that holds it.

In the autumn the ripe acorns
drop from the tree.

As winter comes
food made by the leaves
is stored in the roots
of the oak tree.

The leaves change color,
first gold and then brown.
Leaf stems are sealed shut,
and the leaves get dry.

The dry, brown leaves are dead.
They cannot get water from
the tree's roots.

Some oak trees keep their old leaves
all winter to protect spring buds.

Other oaks drop their leaves when
cold weather comes.
Their leaves cover the acorns
that have not been eaten
or hidden by animals.

Next spring new trees
will start to grow
among strong old ones.

A TREE, and all other plants as well, are vital to life because they can do what animals (except for a few primitive forms) cannot do. Animals must eat plants or other animals, but plants make their own food. Chlorophyll in green leaves enables the plant to produce carbohydrates when sunlight, air and water are present. In the process, plants take in carbon dioxide from the air and return oxygen, thus benefiting animal life in a second way.

The oak tree pictured here is one of many oaks found in temperate climates. It is an English oak, somewhat similar to the American white oak. Leaves differ from one kind of oak to another, as do acorns, but the trees generally have strong central trunks. Their wood is prized for its strength and grain. While animals from insects to deer eat acorns, they are not often thought of as human food. Native Americans, however, ground acorns to make flour.

Oaks are wind-pollinated plants. Their period of flowering is very short, a few days in early spring before leaves mature. The male and female flowers grow separately, and neither has petals, which would only be in the way as wind carries drifts of pollen from tree to tree. Oaks grow in groves or woods because trees must be close enough to permit wind pollination.

Insects and man are the enemies of the oak. Insects lay eggs in acorns as they are forming or on the leaves or tree trunks, causing diseased growths called galls. While deer may browse on seedlings, it is humans who cut trees for commmercial use or to clear land for farming and new communities. Oaks grow slowly, and some old ones survive in parks and protected wildlife areas.

If children cannot observe an oak, they can find other trees to examine for their leaves, bark, how they branch, their flowering and seeds. They can take part in conservation: watering in dry weather, tree planting and being careful not to break branches or injure tree trunks. Sometimes it's an adopt-a-city tree project, belonging to an organization with a name such as Tree People, which makes children conscious of trees and conservation.